Body

Language

for

Success

Alicia Cuello

from information contained in this book or from any programs or document that may accompany it.

Dedication

This book is dedicated to all the angels in disguise who wouldn't let me give up and had blinding faith in me when I didn't. Thank you!

I also want to thank my mom and sisters: Mom, Caroline, Deanna, Elena and Camille. No matter how "left of the middle" my approach to life has been, they never tried to talk me out of anything. I'm sure they questioned my sanity behind closed doors, but in front of me, it was nothing short of 100% support. I couldn't have gotten this far without them. Bear hugs. I love you gals infinity!

Alicia

"Who you are speaks so loudly, I can't hear what you're saying." - Emerson

About this book

We interact with one another on a daily basis. Our conversations run from the mundane, "How's the weather?" to the more serious, "Why is there a dent in my car door?" Each of us is tasked with being able to determine what the other party is really saying (verbally and non-verbally) which includes assessing if they are telling us the truth. It's up to you to be able to determine if you can accept their answer at face value or you need to ask more questions. The book you have in your hands is a quick reference guide for individuals interested in learning basic information on body language. The great thing about this guide is you can seamlessly use the information in both your personal and professional lives.

Writing this book marks a new chapter in my professional life. At this writing, I have decided to leave Corporate America and a steady paycheck. I am also leaving behind being a veteran of 6-layoffs as a Human

Resources Professional.   But this time it's different because this time I have decided to follow my passion and teach other people the power and importance of observation and active listening by using body language. When you take the time to gather the information, a more complete understanding of the person you are dealing with will emerge.

Considering how often we need to interact and even depend on others, it is up to each one of us to be the expert on human behavior. I believe it is imperative for everyone to use body language when interacting with people. Why? Because human beings have the ability to think and rationalize their responses; this includes the ability to lie. However, we do not have control over our body language gestures, that's controlled by the subconscious portion of the brain. Body language signals are responses to real and/or perceived threats to the person and "tip off" a change in emotion in the other party. But don't panic. Just remember, when you see a change, and depending on the subject you're discussing, it could be a talking point (red flag) for you to gather more information. You can easily do this by asking simple and direct questions and then placing the information into context. When you use this approach, you'll be amazed at what happens. And, people will be blown away by the amount of information you can get when they've been struggling to find the same answers.

About the Author

I spent over 20-years in Human Resources. I loved it until I climbed the Human Resources ladder to the point where I was responsible for investigating all interpersonal complaints and/or conflicts within my territory, which happened to be the western half of the country. The complaints varied in severity from simple personality conflicts to serious allegations such as sexual harassment. My other responsibilities included working with the Legal Department on responses to government agency inquiries (EEOC, DOL, etc.) who were also investigating employee complaints, all the while handling day-to-day Human Resources duties which included recruitment, training and development and special projects. It was a lot for one person, and burnout happened quickly.

Within about three to four years I found myself struggling to report to work and once there, dreading the next phone call or visit from a co-worker because it was usually a complaint that needed my immediate attention. Very rarely were the calls or visits from someone who had nice things to say about their co-workers, me or the company. With burnout came a loss of enthusiasm for a career I once loved. I realized I needed to reignite my passion for this profession and decided to become a certified graphologist (a.k.a. handwriting analysis). This certification gave me greater insight into the people I interacted with because I was able to create a personality profile that outlined the writer's habits and tendencies "most likely to occur under pressure." That's valuable information!

People act differently under stress and in some cases, such as an Emergency Room Nurse, a babysitter, or a CEO, reacting poorly under stress can be detrimental to everyone. While most people find this certification "fascinating"—and those "happy hour analysis'" got me more than one free night out of the town — I quickly found out not many U.S. organizations were interested in this skill set. Had I lived in Europe, where it's common practice in the interviewing and hiring process (recruitment), I would have been in business! However, because I lived in the United States, I needed to reflect further on what I could do with my professional skills. By this time in my life, I was in the middle of a mid-life crisis. I was at a point in my life where I decided I could no longer work in such a stressful department. It was then I made the decision to start laying the ground work to leave my profession and try something new.

During this second period of discovery, I decided to "fine tune" my skills and started studying various law enforcement techniques. I was shocked at how few techniques I knew, and I was supposed to be the "the go-to person" for how to conduct an investigation! Armed with the new knowledge, not only did I recognize body language indicators, now I also understood some of the psychology behind the responses. I found it fascinating.

I was also fortunate enough to be in a position where I could directly apply the new techniques I was reading about into my day-to-day investigations. Subsequently, I was able to narrow the group down and determine which were the most practical to use in a day-to-day setting. I also used this approach in my personal life and was amazed at what people attempted to get away with. As all of this was happening, a friend of mine approached me and said she thought I was very good at helping other people understand body language. She also suggested I start giving classes on the subject. As we talked, I commented, "It didn't occur to me that other people didn't see and hear the world the way I do." She laughed and said, "Are you kidding me? Most people are so engrossed in their electronic gadgets and themselves, they forget to pay attention. People need to be reminded how they're coming across has as much of an impact on the situation as the other person's body language; and most people are completely unaware of this. Think of all the times people see one body language gesture, jump to a conclusion, and get really upset with each other. All because of what's being communicated, intentionally or unintentionally, with their body language. You of all people know you should be showing people why body language is so important, how to understand what's really being said, including show people how to better protect themselves and their love ones from people who don't have their best interest at heart."

She made a lot of sense. That was all the encouragement I needed. I was off and running. I quickly found myself teaching body language classes at a variety of venues throughout Denver, Colorado which included local universities, professional organizations, and adult learning institutions. What surprised me most was the number of participants who said they knew very little about body language; including other Human Resources Professionals.

I think one of the most interesting examples came from a couple that met me through one of my courses. For some time, they had been having major renovations done on their home. However, for every good experience they had with a contractor, they would have another equally bad experience. After 2-years of renovations, the home was nowhere near being complete; they were at their wits end. On a whim, the wife asked if I would sit in on the contractors interviews and went on to comment; there was one in particular they really liked "on paper." According to her, he had been referred to them by a client and seemed like a good fit. When I met the contractor, I was immediately struck by his charisma and his ability to come across as the "perfect fit" for the job. My guard went up immediately.

Don't get me wrong, charisma is a great attribute to have. Heck! I have a little bit of it. On the bright side, someone with charisma can "move mountains" because people like them, want to please them, and at times will follow them without asking question. But there's also a dark side to this characteristic – blinding loyalty. I know I'm not the only person who has fallen "under the spell" of a charismatic person or leader who did not have their best interest at heart. Speaking from experience, the results can be detrimental. Because of this, I have learned to recognize "its charisma," take a step back, evaluate the situation, and give my trust only after it's earned. If you take nothing else from this book, always trust your gut! Your gut is your internal alarm system that's telling you something's not right with the situation. More on this later.

When you're dealing with someone who has charisma, keep in mind; emotions color perception and it didn't matter if I liked the contractor on a personal level or not, this was business and I needed to stay focused. I asked the couple not to divulge why I was there (to watch and listen). However, if asked, they were to say I was visiting for the afternoon. The contractor arrived on time and immediately took control of the situation. He started the interview by walking around their home using grant gestures to explain and demonstrate what he would do. As I watched and listened to him, he started to mimic how the husband stood, talked and claimed to have had some of their problems at his house. What he was doing is called mirroring; it's when someone mimics another person in order to connect and appear to be "just like them." We "like" people "like" us and buying is based on emotion. Therefore if my clients "liked him" and he appeared to be "like them", he was more likely to get the contract. He also kept repeating how he "was their contractor" as he continued to make the comment. Over time, I saw my clients start to nod their heads "yes." This guy was good. He was conditioning them to view him already in place, not under consideration. While I understand a good sales person is able to show you how they add value and can solve the problem, his behavior was too much and it made me even more on edge. As the tour of the home ended they asked for references. That was when I saw a crack in his personality. Before the question, he had spoken with confidence and ease, responding effortlessly to the questions they asked. Now he stumbled to explain why he didn't have a list of references with him. He also looked away, whereas before he made eye contact when he answered questions. Hmmmmmmm, my spidey-tingles went into overdrive and it was time to ask a few questions.

Always remember; when asking questions, have the mind set of being in "fact finding mode" only. In the beginning of any situation, you will not have enough information to come to a solid conclusion about what is happening. This is why it's very important your body language, including your voice, remain neutral. Your behavior will influence how the other party responds to you. If they think you are accusing them of something, including lying, they may stop responding or even worse; give you half answers that drag out the question and answer session you're having. With this in mind, and in a neutral tone, I asked the following questions:

- I didn't tell you this before, but I recently had a few home improvement projects completed at my house. So, I'm a little familiar with the process and I have a few questions for you. I know you told us earlier, but how long did you say you have been in business?
- What types of references do you have - personal or professional?
- Would any of your references be available to speak with my clients right now?
- What were the last five complaints you received and how did you resolve them?
- Is there somewhere locally my clients would see a sample of your work?

It was clear the contractor did not like my questions. The more I attempted to get answers, the more evasive his responses became. He then asked in a rather tense voice; "Why are you asking all these questions? This is between the home owners and me. As their contractor, I'm happy to answer **their** questions." Hmmmmm, if I'm asking standard questions in a neutral tone –why was he getting mad at me? There was another red flag. At that point, as my clients started to ask him similar questions, he glanced at his watch, commented he had another appointment and said he would email them a list of references. He also said he would ask one of his customers if my clients could view his work, then he left. My initial thought was, why didn't he have any of it with him? After he left, I explained to my clients all the red flags I was picking up on:

- Charismatic person
- Mirroring
- Stumbling for a response when asked about references
- Not answering my questions. Then appearing to get upset with me for asking them a second time.
- Why didn't he have reference information with him?
- He left before he gave them any answers

I encouraged them to check professional references only, look at some of his work and research his reputation on-line before they went any further with him. I also let them know that I didn't like the guy nor did I trust him. In my opinion they needed to keep looking. I found out later that the contractor had called back with a story that explained away my clients concerns. They claim to have called his references and got the impression they were speaking to his family members instead of professional non-biased references. However, because they liked him, they ignored their suspicion and hired him. Fast forward 6-months, not only did the contractor do poor work (electrical sockets covered up with dry wall, wrong paint colors, uneven tile work, etc.), they found out later that he had used some of their deposit to cover the cost on another job and he had a couple of pending lawsuits filed against him for poor and incomplete work. My clients subsequently fired him (he kept their deposit) and then had to wait until they could save up more money to hire another contractor to finish the work. Ouch, what a painful and costly misstep.

With this story in mind, I'm happy to present a reference guide on some of the more common body language gestures you may encounter. This book can also be used by anyone wanting to increase their ability to connect and communicate better while also recognizing when you might be dealing with a case of dishonesty.   This   includes   homeowners,   HR professionals, small business owners and even parents.

Table of Contents

Body Language Overview

When people find out what my career is, a number of ideas about body language come to mind. Some of them are pretty funny and others make me wonder for the person I'm speaking to. What these conversations tell me is there are a lot of misconceptions about body language. These misconceptions can lead to confusion, inaccurate conclusions, and a lot of misunderstandings that lead to damaged or broken relationships – both personally and professionally. This is one of the reasons I've written this book. My goal is for you to become a better communicator while also understanding what others are really communicating to you, or not. Below are the top five myths I will dispel:

- I'm a mind reader;

- Body language isn't real;

- Body language is only gestures;

- One gesture tells the entire story;

- I can teach you to be a human lie detector;

By the end of this book, I promise you you'll know why these are body language myths.

Spoken word = 10% of conversation=$.10 of every dollar earned

Body language is more than gestures. It's actually a combination of gestures, the voice, how you speak, and everything else. Everything else includes gestures such as the expression on a person's face, nervous "quirks," the way a person appears and how he/she walks; even the way they maintain their personal space. Body language is all encompassing and everything about you is a reflection on who you are as a person. Pretty cool - huh?

Numbers vary, but research suggests once a person leaves a conversation, the spoken word only accounts for about 7% of what is retained. Your voice (i.e. tone, rate of speaking, volume, verbiage used, etc.) accounts for almost 40% of what is taken from the conversation, which leaves over 50% for behaviors such as posture, dressing, nervous tics, and much more. Think of it this way, for every dollar you earn, when you ignore or fail to take into account body language, you're leaving over $.90 on the table.

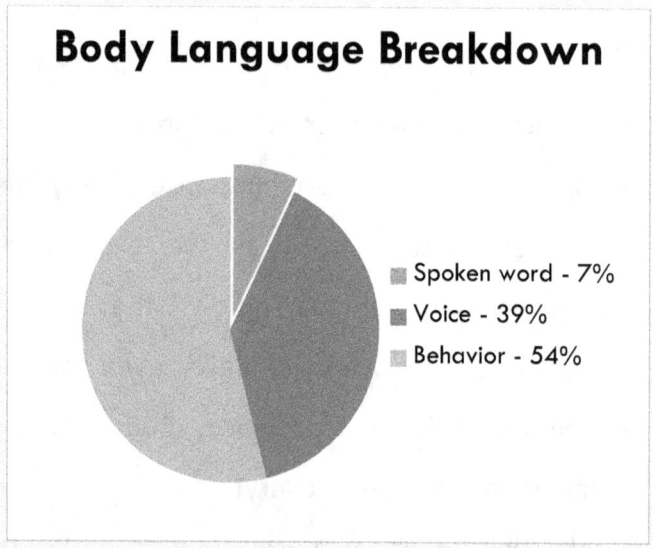

Body Language Breakdown

Spoken word - 7%
Voice - 39%
Behavior - 54%

To get a better understanding of how and what body language is, here's a quick overview. From a very broad perspective, the brain can be divided into three parts: the reptilian, the neo-cortex, and the limbic system. Body language is a product of two of these sections, the neo-cortex and the limbic systems. The speaking portion of the brain (the neo-cortex) controls our conscious responses. It allows human beings to rationalize and respond to a situation. This portion of the brain also gives us the ability to lie. However, body language gestures are overseen by the subconscious portion of the brain (the limbic system). As its name suggests, we have no control over how our bodies respond to an uncomfortable situation. This portion of the brain responds to the world around us and it's always on alert for real or perceived danger. Because we have no control over our reactions, body language gestures are considered the more "honest" response.

Body language interpretation is hard-wired into all human beings and was one of the first ways we learned to communicate with each other as a specie. While we now mostly communicate through language, we also still rely on reading body language signals (both consciously and unconsciously) as a safety mechanism. Consider it our internal alarm system and it's extremely accurate; its job is to keep you safe. Think of it this way, you know when you approach a dark alley or a person and the hair on the back of your neck stands up? That's your body's way of telling you it senses a threat. Or, have you ever watched a colony of ground hogs; one is always on the lookout for danger. The other members of his colony are completely in tune with his behavior. When he senses danger, his behavior changes immediately. This in turn causes the other members of the group to run for cover. That's what your subconscious is doing, but more subtly.

How to use this book

The tips are written in a progressive style. Each tip builds on the previous one. If you read a word that you're not familiar with, know that it will be explained shortly. For example, I reference "norm" several times before I actually explain what this is. I've written the tips in this format so that you are learning from the ground up. In order to become more proficient at body language, you need to have a solid foundation. Now that you have an understanding of body language and how to use this book, let's get started.

The Process:
Be subtle

Never tell the other party you're reading their body language.

What a quick way to end a conversation? Tell someone you're trying to read their body language. While most people are fascinated with the subject, and think "it's great" when it's happening to someone else, they tend to become uncomfortable when it's happening to them and feel "watched." More importantly, if they know they are being watched, you will not be able to get a good read on what's normal behavior for them. Determining their "norm" is extremely important. Without it, you won't be able to correctly interpret what is happening in the situation. Here's how this works.

> *Never tell the other party you're reading their body language.*

I have an outgoing personality and when I need to get to know someone, I can turn on the charm and talk to just about anyone. I like to start my conversations by talking about something light, such as the weather or the drive over; however, if its football season, talking about the Denver Broncos is a given. From there, I'll ask the other party to tell me about themselves. Within a few minutes, we're having a great conversation. As they become relaxed and are talking about something familiar, I notice their body language, how they are standing, their tone of voice, the direction they are facing, etc.) and I make sure I note behaviors that are specific to them such as playing with their hair or a ring or maybe they have their arms crossed. I drink it all in because it's possible this is just the way they behave." While most people would assume crossed arm as a sign that someone is closed off, I instead recognize it's possible this is their "norm," however I won't know this until I spend a few minutes talking to them about a subject that they feel relaxed talking about, such as themselves. At one point or another, the conversation usually turns to what each one of us does for a living. I always go last...for a reason.

When they heard what I specialize in, most of the time, it stresses them out and I can see immediate changes in their behavior. Such as, their size may shrink or as they cover their torso with an arm or a drink and the tone in their voice screams distress as they respond, "Really? Does that mean you can tell what I'm thinking?" Unfortunately, now that the other person is stressed out, they start to exhibit behaviors that aren't normal and could easily be misconstrued to mean something else by another person. The outcome may or may not have a negative impact on the situation. However, because I placed their reaction into context (more on this later), I realize this normal and I have nothing to worry about. Instead, I quickly add, "I'm off the clock and unless I'm being paid, I don't make it a habit to read other people's body language." For the most part, that's a true statement. However, there are some behaviors I can't ignore, I automatically "see and hear" them. After reading this book, don't be surprised if you experience that as well.

First Impressions, Self-Awareness & Connecting

You have 7-seconds to make a great first impressions. That's one second less than the attention span of a gold fish.

First impressions can make or break a situation. When I work with job seekers and leaders, I can't stress this enough. Here's what happens within 7-seconds of seeing and/or meeting someone, we all make sweeping judgements about one another. Then we spend the rest of the conversation looking for statements and/or behaviors that support our initial conclusion about the other person. It's called confirmation bias and it's another of those evolutionary things that are a holdover from long ago. Oh! And we

> *You have 7-seconds to make a great first impressions. That's one second less than the attention span of a gold fish.*

tend to look for characteristics we value in ourselves. By the way, it can take months to overcome a bad first impressions and even more interesting, we tend to not forget our first impressions. So, why am I bringing this up? Because, other people's first impression with you will influence the way they interact with you. Keep in mind that some of the areas you are judged on include: success, success potential, social-economy status, education, and being trustworthy.

We tend to forget how we are coming across to others not only visually but also vocally. Spend some time determining what your norms are when you're relaxed and when you're under stress. You might be surprised to find out what parts of you, including the voice, change when you're under stress. To help you determine your norm, I have included a form called "What's My Norm?" in the appendix of this book. You will need to work with a partner over the course of a few days. The partner will watch and listen to you at various times throughout the day and note your behaviors on the form. Once you review the findings, you may want to modify your behavior. Sometimes you may need to come across as more assertive, sometimes less assertive.

The image you want to project will depend on the situation. Changing behaviors takes time. The first step is to have the behavior brought to your attention, and then make a conscious effort to come across differently.

When I'm working with sales professionals, one of the best ways to bump up their "it" factor, and come across as successful and trustworthy is to emulate someone who is their definition of success. For example, I had one attendee, who was ex-military, told me he really admired how his Commander always kept his composure and was able to effortlessly influence the troop. However, at times he came across as lacking in warmth. As we both identified other people he really admired and who had warmth, we were able to combine the two personalities into the exact way he wanted people to view him. From there, I had him write down, remember, and watch (if he had video), these people in action. Then pretend he was them before he went into a sales call. He was to think about how they would sit, talk, carry themselves, dress, and behave. I find this approach to be extremely successful. When I'm giving talks on first impressions, I always ask the audience to close their eyes and think about James Bond. I ask them to hear the music, see him walk into a room, look at what he's wearing, his stare, etc. Then I ask them to sit like they are James Bond. I'm always amazed to see the change in the room. Most people sit up taller, some smile, but most of all there is an air of confidence that wasn't in the room before. Now, I also remind them, James is a cold blooded killer, and they are going to use him, they need to also throw in a dash of warmth and humanity – maybe an Oprah Winfrey or a George Clooney. By using this exercise, what you're doing is creating a "cluster" of positive body language cues. This way when someone only catches one cue, it's a positive one and it leaves a lasting impact.

Take a look at the pictures below. The picture on the left was taken at the start of the meeting. As the meeting progressed, she changed her behavior (norm) dramatically (i.e., her expression, the tilt of her head, and her arms):

Ask yourself this, does she come across as "neutral"? Not in my opinion. As the party wanting and needing information, it's your job to stay

Emotion colors your understanding of a situation..

neutral. If you find yourself starting to become emotional about a situation, be careful. Emotion colors perception. Once it appears you have already made up your mind, the other person may be less inclined to participate in the conversation especially if the outcome isn't in their favor. Take a break and if need be, reschedule the conversation for later in the day or tomorrow.

Norms

A person's "norm" is how he/she naturally stands or sits when

> In order to determine a person's norm, they need to be able to relax and trust you.

relaxed. As stated earlier, it's extremely important to determine their norm before you start collecting body language signals. Without it, your interpretation of their body language will be off. The trick is; in order to determine a person's norm, they need to be able to relax and trust you. The easiest way to accomplish this is to find something the two of you have in common. How? By spending a few minutes *talking*. For example, I live in Colorado and most people are involved in some type of winter sport. When I meet someone during winter, I talk about winter sports such as snowboarding, skiing or snow shoeing. Once I find the "link" we have in common (skiing, snow shoeing), I talk about the subject. Because the two of us now have this sport "in common" and the subject is neutral (meaning neither one of us has anything to hide around the subject), I'm now seeing as just like them. And we naturally want to trust someone who's just like us, because we're good people right? Therefore, they must be too. Subconsciously, now the other party is starting to trust me and is free to relax. At that point, I can determine their "relaxed norm." Remember, this is what the contractor did while he was interacting with my clients; he gave the appearance of being "just like them" by claiming to have experienced the same problems as them. As a result of this, my clients started to trust him and buy into what he was saying. Here is the key to this approach; you have to be sincere. If you're not, the other person will pick up on it and actually trust you less which will impede your ability to figure out what's normal for them. Once you've found this link, another way to increase your trust factor even more is to use mirroring.

Mirroring is when you "mimic" the other person's behavior. Normally, it's subconscious and just happens when people are in sync, a lot of times we don't even realize we're mirroring each other until after the fact. However, subconsciously the two of us have already connected – and that can be good or bad. For example, watch couples as they walk; couples who are doing well will walk in sync; the same stride. On the opposite, watch two people arguing; sport is a great example of this. When one person shouts and places their hands on their hips, so does the other person.

However, when you need to consciously mirror someone, be subtle. My advice; pick two behaviors (MAX) to mimic. My focus goes to behaviors to mimic; how quickly they speak and one physical behavior. For example, if they smile, I smile. If they cross their legs, I cross my legs. I mimic the behavior a few seconds after them. Otherwise, it becomes obvious and it ruins my credibility. This is also the technique the contractor used with my clients. They fell for it, I was suspicious because he mirrored too many of their mannerisms.

Once you've connected with the other person, spend a few minutes observing how the person talks and holds themselves. I like to use a technique I call the 4-part body observation. I take the body and break it down into four parts: the head/face; the voice; the torso; and legs/feet. Also keep in mind, sometimes people have quirks or gestures that are normal for them. For example, did you ever watch the TV series, "Boston Legal?" They had a character called, "Hands." This was a character who walked around with his hands on his legs. While it looks odd, when you get to know the character, it isn't "odd", it is just him; i.e. his norm. However, you don't know that until you spend some time with him. In that case, you would make a note of it and keep talking.

The other point to keep in mind is, when someone is under stress, they will also have habits or "ticks" (and so will you) that will be part of their "stress norm." Once they are out of the stressful situation or become comfortable in the conversation, these "ticks" will disappear or subside. You need to note both the relaxed and the stress behaviors. For example, look at the picture below. If I were to meet this person, I would spend a few minutes speaking with him. Once I felt he was relaxed, I would note the following:

- Head/facial expression: neutral, head slightly tilted;

- Voice: I'll need to wait until he speaks, then note several attributes such as volume, tone, pauses;
- Torso: facing me; hands on hips;
- Feet: one foot facing me one foot slightly turned out

Now that you have this information, it's time to move into the questions you

Body language is how a person *feels* about a situation.

have for the situation you're working on. After each question, you will be watching and listening for changes in their norm. A change in behavior is a signal for a "change in emotion" also known as a hot spot/red flag talking point; remember body language is how a person *feels* about a situation. When you see or hear a red flag, know that something made the other party feel differently and depending on the subject, it may or may not be time for you to ask more questions to determine why the change.

Body Observation
The face – universal emotions

Body language researcher, Dr. Paul Ekman, is given credit for determining there are seven universal emotions: happy, sad, surprise, disgust, fear, anger and contempt. Once you learn to recognize each emotion, you can go anywhere in the world and also know how a person truly feels about the subject. Of the seven, I consider the two most damaging to be anger and contempt. Both will be discussed in greater detail than the others. Here are the first five emotions:

Happiness	• Both lip corners pulled up and toward the ears (vs. toward the back of the jaw). • Crow's feet around the eyes. • Narrow eye openings.
Sadness	• Lip corners down and mouth hangs open. • Eyelids heavy.

	• Inner corner eyebrows turned up. • When faking sadness, turning the inner eyebrows up is one of the most difficult movements to make. The model was unable to recreate this emotion.
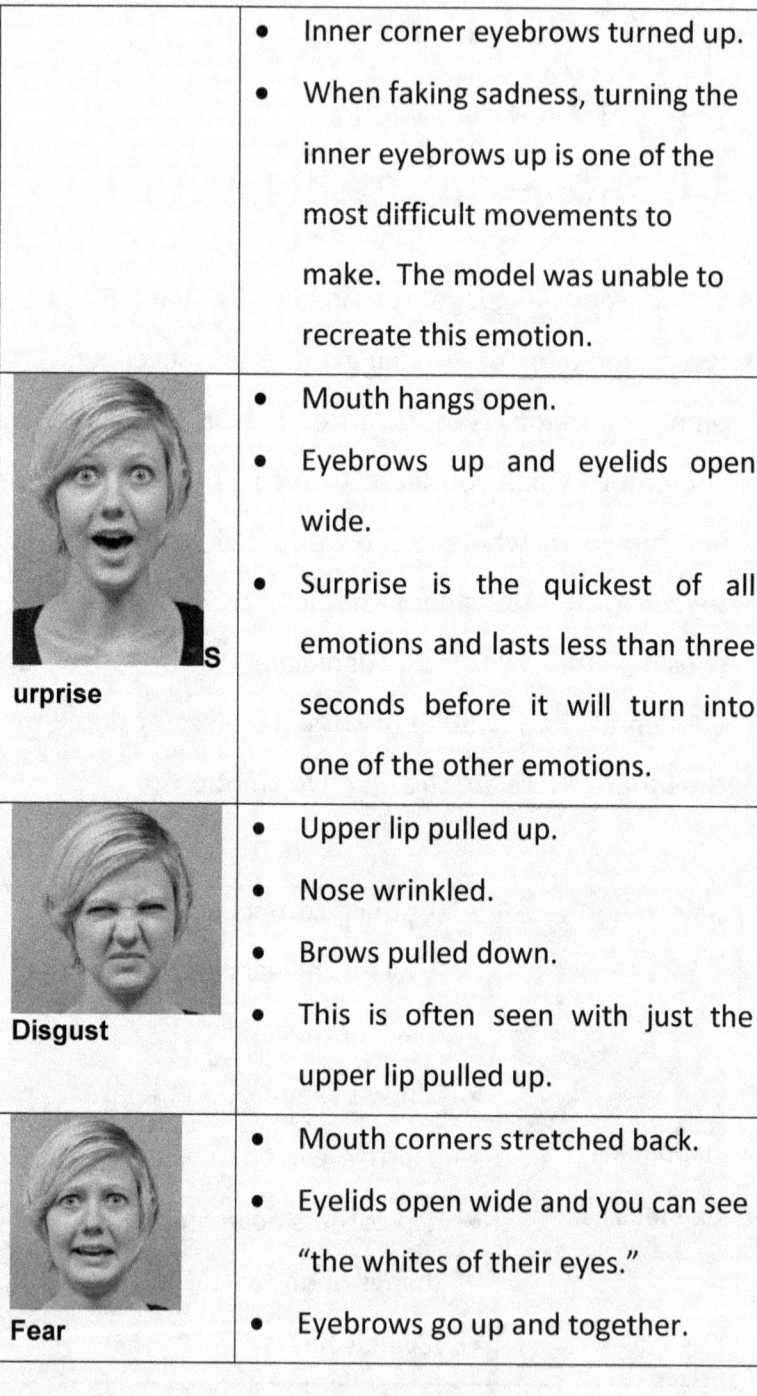urprise	• Mouth hangs open. • Eyebrows up and eyelids open wide. • Surprise is the quickest of all emotions and lasts less than three seconds before it will turn into one of the other emotions.
Disgust	• Upper lip pulled up. • Nose wrinkled. • Brows pulled down. • This is often seen with just the upper lip pulled up.
Fear	• Mouth corners stretched back. • Eyelids open wide and you can see "the whites of their eyes." • Eyebrows go up and together.

Learn to recognize anger

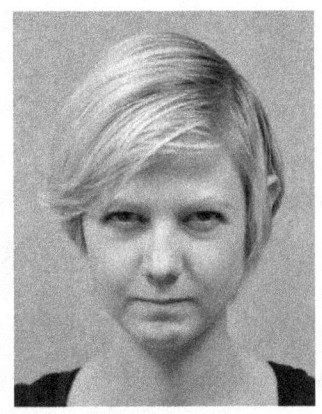

Anger is reflected with the following mannerisms: Lips narrow, red part of lip rolled in tight; lower and upper eyelids pulled up; eyebrows

> Anger is a universal emotion and at times it's appropriate.

pulled down; may flash teeth. Anger is a universal emotion and at times it's appropriate. It's important to recognize anger and place it into context (more on this later). For example, I ask a candidate about their last boss and I see a flash of anger. As I listen closely to the details of the candidate's explanation on the relationship, I also watch out for additional gestures to determine what's going on internally with the candidate.

Then I phrase my follow up questions based on where I saw and heard red flags in his/her body language responses.

For example, I once interviewed a very animated candidate who spoke clearly and articulate, and appeared happy to be interviewing for the job. That changed once she explained her resignation from the last employer. She claimed she resigned due to unethical behavior on her manager's part and the company's failure to look into her claim. She also said the company retaliated against her by refusing to pay her unemployment claim. As she spoke, her facial expression and tone of voice reflected how angry she was with the company, at the work environment and their refusal to pay her unemployment claim. However, as she relayed the portion of the story about the State awarding her unemployment claim, her entire demeanor changed again. She went from being very animated and communicative to soft spoken, she no longer made eye contact, instead she looked down, and started to rub her hands together. Then she handed me her unemployment paperwork from the State. It turned out her employer decided not to fight her claim, instead choosing not to attend the hearing; subsequently, she received her unemployment benefits. Once I explained this, she returned to the outgoing candidate she had been at the start of her interview. Was her anger at the company warranted? Probably. While I can't speak to the claim of unethical behavior, if I had resigned for what I believed was a legitimate reason and then the company attempted to deny my unemployment claim, I would have been angry too. What this experience reinforced to me is the need to always ask extra questions when you see and hear red flags, especially anger.

Learn to recognize contempt (i.e., smirking)

The look of contempt is expressed by one lip corner pulled in and back on one side of face resembling a half-smile. According to Wikipedia, the definition for contempt is a mix of disgust and anger. Robert Solomon places contempt on the same continuum as resentment and anger and argues the difference between the three is that resentment is directed toward a higher status individual; anger is directed toward an equal status individual; and contempt is directed toward a lower status individual. As a representative of the Human Resources Department, I've experienced all three and for the most part, I take it in stride. The exception to this rule is when I see this emotion during a serious subject matter.

For example, during one interview I caught a flash of anxiety on the candidate's face as she was asked why she left her last employer. Towards the end of the interview, I brought up the subject up again and explained it was me, but I didn't understand why she left her last employer (her explanation didn't make sense). Her response was to flash a look of contempt at me, crossed her legs and clasps her hands around her knees and replied in a condescending tone, "Why is this so hard to understand? Even my husband understood how their system worked...." During this brief exchange, I counted four red flags around the topic of why she left her last employer: a flash of anxiety, look of contempt, crossed her legs, clasped her hands around her knees, and a condescending tone that conveyed to me, non-verbally, "Wow, you're stupid and I'm smarter than you." Hmmmm, interesting.

Aren't people you're meeting for the first time, especially job candidates, supposed to be on their best behavior? If someone flashes the look of contempt, at the beginning of your interactions with them, what do you think they will act like once they feel comfortable in the situation and/or position? In a collaborative setting, contempt can ruin a team dynamics. Within a personal relationship, it's just as damaging. When someone thinks they are better than you, you are going to have a hard time getting them to change their opinion. And most times, you won't be able to change their opinion. By the way, we didn't hire her.

The Voice

The voice accounts for almost 40% of what a person takes from a conversation. This is where the expression, "It's not what you said, it's how you said it" came from.

The voice accounts for almost 40% of what a person takes from a conversation.

When you first start to work with the voice it can seem overwhelming because there are so many areas you can focus in on. To simply the process here are the three areas I think are the easiest to work with:

Volume:

In general there are three levels: soft, medium, and loud. All three are easy to determine. Here's an interesting titbit; when someone becomes excited, their voice naturally becomes louder. Louder could indicate happy or angry. However, when they become embarrassed or ashamed, the voice naturally drops. For example, have you ever spoken to a child that knew they had been busted doing something they shouldn't have?

What happens when you go to speak to them? They tend to look down and speak softly right? That's what I'm talking about. As adults we do it too.

Rate of speech

How quickly you speak reflects how quickly you process information. Here's a suggestion for you, when you're meeting someone for the first time, slow down your rate of speech until you're able to determine the other person's speed. Why? Because it builds trust and it non-verbally shows respect to the other person. People need to understand you before they will trust you. Once you determine someone's rate of speech, mimic/mirror their rate of speech. If they talk fast, speak faster. By speaking fast the other person is telling you they process information very quick and they want you to get to the point. If they speak slowly, slow it down. This person is telling you non-verbally they process information slowly. If you speak too slowly for the fast speaker or too fast for the slow speaker, you will end up frustrating them. The fast speaker will be frustrated because they need you to get to the point and you're taking up too much time. The slow speaker will become frustrated because they were not able to follow you because you were giving them too many details too quickly. By matching the other person's rate of speech, you are showing them respect and increasing your trust factor. Plus, when they change their rate of speech (i.e. red flag), you'll be able to recognize the sooner because you're mirroring them.

Tone

I've read some experts believe the tone of voice accounts for 35-40% of the message you're sending. Think about that. Some are friendly and pleasant and

> Some experts believe the tone of voice accounts for 35-40% of the message you're sending.

others can be hard and off putting. Whatever tone you use has a direct impact on how people perceive you. The tone also tells you the emotion behind the words. Think about the last time you hear a really great speaker. By using the right tone, the speaker was able to convey authority, their conviction behind their words and deliver a message that stayed with the audience. That's the power of listening to tone of voice.

As you start to listen to tone in someone's voice, you'll be able to quickly determine how they feel about the situation and possibly the person they're talking to. For example, I used to work with a manager whose undertone had an undercurrent of anger, but only when talking to certain people. Yet when anyone talked to him about this, he claimed to have no idea he came across that way. I believe him; remember most of body language is done subconsciously. Here's the interesting part, his tone changed depending on whether or not the person was a valued worker or not. Or, if the situation was becoming heated and not going his way, you could hear the anger rising in his voice. Funny thing was, he didn't see or hear it. Over time, everyone came to know that was his "norm" and when to give him space all based on how he sounded on the phone. Another interesting titbit on the tone; depending on what word you emphasize in a sentence can change the way you come across in a situation. For example, place emphasis on the BOLDED word in the sentences below:

- I had a **great** time at the venue and concert.

- I had a great time at the **venue** and concert.

- I had a great time at the venue and **concert**.

Did you notice how it changed the message you were conveying? In the first sentence you had a great time overall; in the second you had a good time in at the venue only; and in the third sentence, you had a great time at the concert only. Moral of the story, listen to your tone and the tone of others!

The torso

I love watching people's torso. First of all, it's really easy to watch because it's so big. Secondly, I can also, at a glance, determine how interested the other person is in what I'm saying. Finally, it also tells me when the other person wants out of the conversation. Here's how it works.

When we like something, we naturally want to be closer to the object of our affection. If the other party is comfortable with me, some part of their body will stretch or lean towards me including the torso. When I work with college students on body language and interviewing skills, one of the ways I suggest they show their interest in the position is to lean forward slightly. This is a commonly known sign for interest and most people will recognize it when they see it. Look at the picture below. That picture was taken when I was talking to one of my favorite managers. Note how both of us are leaning towards each other.

The opposite will happen if the conversation is not going well and one or both parties are uncomfortable. Usually what happens is someone will suddenly pull away from the other person. Sometimes, it happens suddenly like they touched something hot, and at other times, it's more subtle and happens slowly. The best part about this is because the torso is so large, a pull away gesture is easy to spot.

The feet

I love the feet. The feet are incredibly expressive, unsuppressed and show a wide range of emotions, from happiness (happy feet), to nervousness (foot turn or chair wrap) to anger (foot tapping or foot stomp). As I started to read books on body language; multiple authors stressed, watch the feet. More than one commented, our society teaches us at young age to suppress the feelings on our face. Children hear comments such as, "Stop making that face," or "Put on your poker face." However, no one ever says, "Put on your poker feet" or "Watch your feet, they may give away weather or not you have a great poker hand," would they? That's why many believe the feet are the most honest body part because they are so expressive and no one watches them! Here's other interesting piece, people tend to have an "out of sight, out of mind" approach to their body parts. Once we believe people can't see what we're doing, that gives us carte blanc to behave in ways we wouldn't normally when we think someone is looking. This includes playing footsy under the table with one of our co-workers when publically that would never happen.

Once I started paying attention to below the table, I was amazed at what went on "down under." Not only did I move my chair into a position where I could see the other party from head to toe, I also made it a point to glance at the feet often. Sometimes when I couldn't see a person's hands or their feet I would subtly or not so subtly drop my pen on the floor in order to look under the table. People had no idea what I was doing and therefore didn't change their behavior – the method was genius! I saw a number of interesting foot behaviors over the years. Here are a couple gestures I saw:

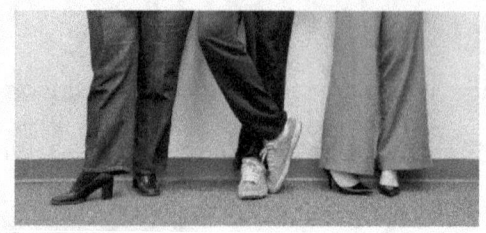

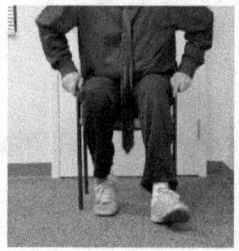
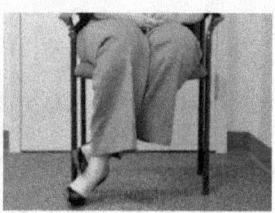

Both men and women also tended to cross their legs when I was talking to them. This is great for you because 1.) You can mimic this gestures causally and 2.) You have a better view of their foot and will notice red flags more easily. Here's what happens, when someone crosses their leg, they have now

> Anytime a behavior causes physical discomfort it's not normal and should be seen as a red flag.

"freed" the foot to more easily express itself. I've seen feet started out kicking slowly, then become faster and faster as their level of stress increases. Once the other person is all out to the uncomfortable topic, the foot either slows down or stops. Don't forget, you have to figure out what is normal feet behavior before you start to notice changes. For example, their norm may be to swing their leg or foot while they're talking. Your red flag happens when there is a change in **that** behavior.

Other interesting foot positions include one foot turning in and the foot wrapped. Both positions are not comfortable (try it and you'll see what I mean) they immediately tipped me off that the subject matter was not welcomed by the other party. Remember, anytime a behavior causes physical discomfort it's not normal and should be seen as a red flag.

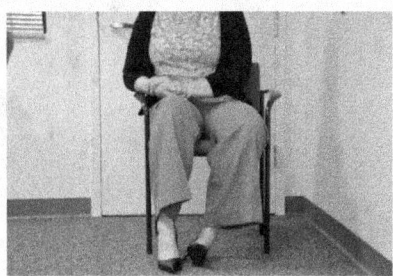

Foot turn

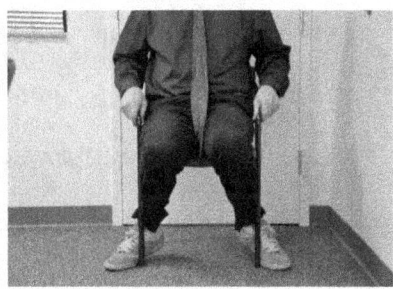

Foot wrap

The last two feet actions were the feet stretching towards me or away from me. Remember when I talked about leaning the torso towards someone is a good thing; well you will also see it in the feet as well. If the person is comfortable with us and the situation, a body part will move closer to us. However, if uncomfortable, they will not.

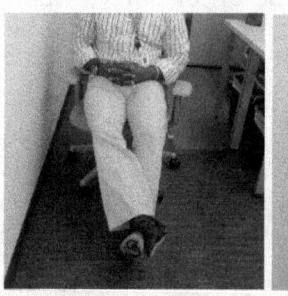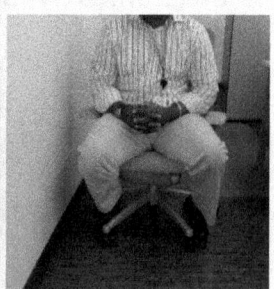

Bonus section

Normally, when I coach individuals who are just starting to use the four part body observation approach, I suggest starting with what I consider to be the easiest parts to read. I believe it's the torso and feet. However, here are two more that I find fascinating to watch.

Bonus tip #1: The nose

The nose touch is being included because it takes a lot of heat for being a sure sign of deception. While it's true when a person becomes agitated, which could include when they're lying, the membrane on the inside of the nose becomes inflamed and starts to itch. While it was an indicator, it doesn't necessarily mean the person is lying. However, a lot of people believe this to be the case. As with any gesture, always put into context and ask more questions.

I personally think this belief got "stuck" in the public's mind due to the Clinton/Lewinsky Interviews. There was a time when multiple body language experts dissected the interview and pointed out how on multiple occasions after Clinton lied, he touched his nose. While Clinton was lying, when other people touch their nose, give them the benefit of the doubt and recognize there are other reasons people touch their nose. Ask yourself: is it hay fever season, do they need to sneeze, or could their nose legitimately itch? Instead of jumping to a conclusion, note a change in the baseline and decide if you need to ask more questions. I used to work in a building I was allergic to. There would be times when I would spend weeks rubbing and/or blowing my nose all day. Once I left the building, I was fine. Remember, sometimes a nose itch is just a nose itch.

Bonus tip #2: Neck exposure

The neck is being included because it's an easy way to determine when someone is comfortable and relaxed. For the most part, our skeletal system protects the majority of our body. An exception to this is the neck area. Attacking this area is one of the easiest ways to harm an individual and as human beings, we are acutely aware of this. When people feel threatened, such as answering why they were let go from their last job, I would sometimes see them touch or attempt to protect this area by touching their neck or playing with a necklace or tie knot. However, once they were in a neutral territory (topic), their hands would leave the neck area. When talking to people, you will know you have succeeded in securing their trust when they expose their neck. Look at the picture below. While the subject has a look of annoyance on his face, he's still willing to participate in the conversation because his head is titled, the neck exposed and he continues to face the other party. That's success!

Bonus tip #3:

Hands move. Depending on the speaker, hands can be very dramatic and expressive especially when used to emphasize a point. Other times our hands give us sense of the calmness through touch. Your hands get a lot of attention because of their ability to cause harm. Subsequently, people (you and I included) spend a lot of time looking at your hands, whether we realize it or not. People want to see your hands. When you hide them it gives the impression you're nervous or you have something to hide. This is one of those gestures that seems to get almost everyone's attention. For example, I recently attended a public speaking seminar where several attendees went on stage to practice their craft. As soon as one of them took to the stage, the first thing I noticed was when a speaker had his hands in his pockets. Not only did I notice it, so did the teacher and I heard one attendee mumble, "Take your hands out of your pockets." Interestingly enough, none of the participants were aware they were doing this. Remember, body language is ruled by the sub-conscious and a lot of the time we are completely unaware of how our body is responding to stress.

When a person has their hand in their pockets, it comes across as less polished or less confident. However, when you place it into context - the speakers were on stage in-front of a group of peers, which is one of the most stressful situations a public speaker can face, this nervous behavior is normal given the situation. Another take away from the experience was the confirmation that people watch your hands!

Two other commonly seen hand positions are: 1. Hands clenched 2. Hands and wrist pointed up like a stop sign.

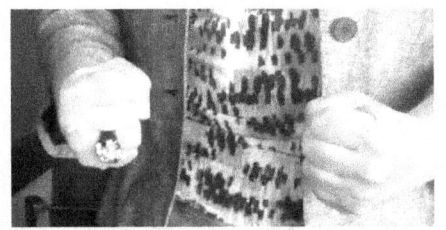

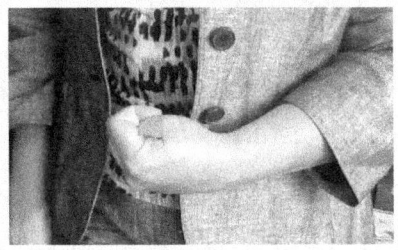

Whenever I see someone start to clench their fists, I recognize this gesture has a number of meaning including possible violence. It can also symbolize happiness (fist pump), or it may be used as a stress reliever (touch). This hand gestures sometimes look like someone squeezing their hands into a fist, releasing, and then repeat. Or they place their thumbs in the ball of their hands. However, if you see someone making a fist and feel threatened in any way, I don't hesitate to stop the conversation.

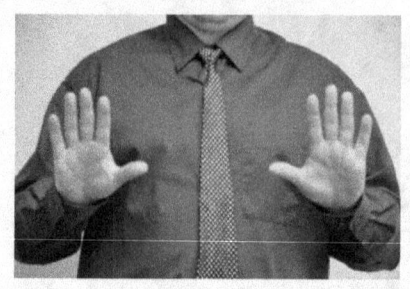

I call the second gesture the "stop sign." Sometimes you will see this gesture while watching a press conference. The speaker, usually a member of law enforcement, gives a brief update then comments as they make this gesture, "I'll now open it up for questions." Do you really believe the speaker wants to answer reporter questions? On the surface, that doesn't appear to be the case. These gestures implies back-off and give me some space; they are symbolically pushing you away. However, when you put the gesture into context (required press conference), it makes sense. The speaker is in the middle of an extremely stressful situation, has limited information to share, yet must hold a press conference and answer questions. Which a number of times the department does not have information ready to be released to the public.

The most neutral (non-threatening) position for the hands are: hands open, palms turned up or to the side, slightly curled and by your side.

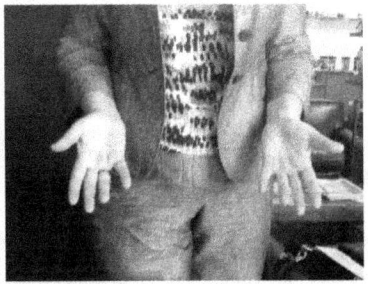

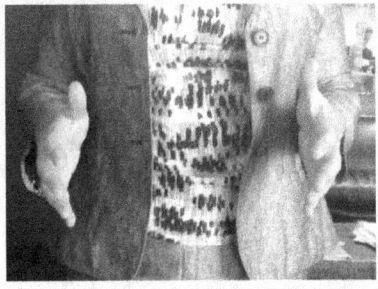

Just remember, when you talking to people keep your hands in view and relaxed. This will automatically raise your trust factor.

Ask and Listen

Ask simple questions

Have you ever had a conversation where all the other person did was fire off question after question before you had a chance to answer them? I think we've all had that experience.

> How many of you have chosen to "forget" to answer the question or didn't answer a question because you were confused? From a body language stand, it's important to know the difference.

How did it make you feel? For me, it usually made me mad and depending on who I was dealing with, I would stop answering the questions on purpose. Whenever I have this experience, I see it in one or two different ways, either the other person has so many questions to ask; they want to make sure they ask all of them at once and have no idea how they were coming across. Or, it's a power play. Personally, I think this type of behavior is both disrespectful and used as a form of intimidation (i.e. look how much smarter I am than you). While I understand the other person has a list of questions they need answered, interrupting and/or talking over someone usually results in the other person becoming upset and/or withdrawn. How many of you have chosen to "forget" to answer the question or didn't answer a question because you were confused? From a body language stand, it's important to know the difference.

As I was studying law enforcement techniques, I learned this is one of their interviewing approaches. They use a party's failure to answer a question, as a hot spot/talking point and are able to zero in on where to ask more questions. Had they chosen to fire off question after question without giving the other party time to respond, and the interviewee failed to answer a question, the interviewer would have no way of knowing if this omission was intentional or the subject became confused and accidently missed the question. Learn from law enforcement, take your time and use missing answers as a hot spot to ask more questions. The next time you need to gather information from someone ask them one question at a time using a neutral voice, wait for their answer and then decide what else you need to ask. For example, you need to ask your teenager what happened to the car's door. Start by asking, "What did you do last night?" Listen to their response, and follow up with, "Have you seen the car's door today?" follow up with, "What happened to the car's door?" By taking this approach, you now have more time to watch and listen to their body language; when you see or hear a flag, that's where you need to ask another question. When you take your time the red flags become more visible.

Active listening

Now more than ever we need to slow down and listen. We live in a society that's "on" 24-hours a day, 7-days a week. At any moment, you can check Facebook, Twitter, Instagram and a variety of other social media to get the latest update on the stock market, your favorite celebrity, company, family or clients. As a result of this, we have a society who is always jockeying for attention and trying to get the last word in a conversation. Unfortunately this behavior has spilled over into daily interactions where you see people interrupting by talking over each other with some even believing screaming is an acceptable way to communicate. All of this is done in an attempt to be heard. That is not active listening nor is it an effective way to have a thoughtful conversation.

Active listening is completely being present when you're in a conversation. It necessitates the ability to halt multi-tasking and/or thinking of a response before the other party stops talking. As the person who needs information, it's in your best interest to refrain from talking or you might miss something important. If you're about to have an important conversation, take a few minutes to write your questions down and then refer back to them throughout the conversation. That way you won't have to worry about forgetting a question and can fully focus on the other party. As they are talking, if they make a comment you want to follow up on, make a note of it on list of questions.

Most people are uncomfortable with silence. Yet I have found if I'm quiet, a lot of people "volunteer" more

> There's power in silence. (Unknown)

information than I asked for. That can be a double edged sword. However, over the years I've come to realize those comments can be a gold mine of information and on more than one occasions, this has helped me make a better decision on their character and on their capabilities.

Pay attention (watch and listen)

I'm always surprised to see how many people spend the majority of the conversation taking notes (if it's an interview), checking their cell phone, or looking around the room while the other person is talking. They are missing all the good stuff!

In reality, they should ask the question then watch and listen for changes to behavior. Only then will you be able to determine at what point additional questions need to be asked. Remember, people can tell you anything you want to hear. But their body will betray them when they are under stress and that includes lying. The body will naturally want to take the least stressful way out of a situation which is, telling the truth. When we lie, it stresses the body out because now not only do we have to remember what we said, we also have to watch to see if you believe us, and if you ask questions, the lie may need to become more elaborate with more details; that will stress any one out.

Here's a perfect example, one day I was interviewing a candidate with another manager. The manager and I had the agreement that she would run the interview and ask the main questions. My job was to listen and observe the responses. As we moved through the interview and the manager took very detailed notes, I focused on the candidate. When the candidate was told the salary budgeted for the position and asked if that amount worked for her, she briefly flashed a look of disgust then pleasantly said, "Yes, that works for me." I let the interview continued and towards the end I asked her again about the salary amount. She turned to look at me, pursed her lips and spoke in a condescending way, "I'm aware of the salary or I wouldn't be here." Now I've noted three red flags around her salary requirements: the flash of disgust, pursed lips, and her condescending tone. Instead of letting it go, I explained how she was the only one who knows if she could live on this amount and I wanted her to think about it overnight. This sparked a longer conversation between the two of us which resulted in her admitting she couldn't live on the salary amount and decided the position wasn't for her. The manager later asked me how I knew to ask her more questions on salary. I explained what had taken place and she admitted she didn't see or hear anything because she was taking notes. My advice to you is to get in the habit of asking a question then watch and listen to the reaction.

If you need a minute or two to digest what the other party was saying or to observe, take it. If they ask what you're doing, explain you're thinking about what they have said; acknowledge you recognize how busy they are and let them know you want to make sure you have all your questions answered before they leave. Once explained your approach isn't seen as a problem. People appreciate clear communication and respect for their time.

Place changes into context

A mistake a lot of people make is the belief that one gesture tells them all the information they need to jump to a conclusion. An example of this is crossed arms.

> Jumping to a conclusion based on one behavior can be damaging and irresponsible.

Unfortunately, when most people see this gesture, they

assume the other party is "closed off" and therefore unapproachable. While that is possible, what if that's the way the person stands naturally. Or maybe they're cold. Jumping to a conclusion based on one behavior can be very damaging and irresponsible.

Many years ago, I was informed "off the record" that several employees, myself included, would be losing their positions within a month. This would be my fourth lay off and I was a semester away from graduating with my Master's Degree. While I was devastated, I also used the time to discreetly clean out my desk and start my job search. By the time I was called into the Director's office, I was ready to lose my job. I chose to show my acceptance of the situation (it was a business decision) by being quiet throughout the meeting. I didn't have any questions to ask and left immediately. Because I didn't have questions (fourth lay off - I could have recited the speech to myself), my Director, who didn't know me very well, took my silence as "rage" at her and the company. After I left, she proceeded to tell multiple people in the Human Resources and Legal Departments that based on my reaction, she was concerned for her safety and the department's safety because she was certain I was going to return and "go postal" on my co-workers. Fortunately, one of the Executives had called to check on me. I let her know I was fine and I had known for weeks my position was being eliminated. She and I ended the conversation by setting up a time to meet for lunch. Shortly thereafter, she received a call from my ex-director who promptly explained her concerns. The Executive didn't waste a minute and immediately took up for me. She informed her of our conversation and also discussed how damaging jumping to conclusions can be. Not only was the Director damaging my reputation (slander), she was also placing the employer at risk because her concern was unwarranted.

Multiple body language experts, including Janine Driver advise to always collect at least 2-3 signals that form a "cluster" of hot spots before arriving at a conclusion. These signals should be a combination of visual changes and/or auditory changes. Never base your determination on one gesture. When you see a change in the baseline (relaxed or stressed), stop and ask yourself: 1. what were the two of you discussing? 2. Is this normal behavior for the situation? If this is normal for the situation, make a mental note. But additional questions might not be necessary. If it's not normal behavior, ask more questions.

To illustrate my first point, had my Director known someone had tipped me off and this was my fourth layoff, she probably would have recognized my silence and lack of questions was normal behavior for someone in my situation. Had this been the reaction from one of the other employees who had never lost their job and didn't know they were being laid off; she should have asked questions in an attempt to discover why they were behaving this way. Nothing is more damaging to a relationship or a reputation than jumping to the wrong conclusion.

R
ed Flags/Hot Spots/Talking Points

If you have ever tried to "lie your way" out of a situation, maybe a speeding ticket? Then you know how stressful it can be. Not only are you trying to think up an explanation "on the fly", you also have to gage if the other party believes you. I've broken down the process into five "easy" steps:

> Lying is
>
> stressful!

- Step 1: Create the lie and keep the charade up.

- Step 2: Convince the person.

- Step 3: Watch and listen to the other person and make sure they're buying your story.

- Step 4: Remember any changes made to the original lie. (Repeat Steps 2&3.)

- Step 5: Monitor all bodily reactions to stressors both verbally and visually. Attempt to suppress or control the response.

That's a lot to be responsible for and the body preferring to live stress free is it's going to find a way to alleviate the stress level. One way or another, the body will automatically use any body language gesture at its disposal including disruptions to the voice (speech pattern, volume, tone, etc.), nervous ticks, and bodily responses (i.e. sweating, shallow breathing, etc.). Now let's discuss a few techniques.

Trust your gut

I recently read a study that claims the subconscious processes 40,000 non-verbals in 40 seconds. However, only a

> If it sounds "off," it probably is.

small portion of the information is deemed important enough to be brought to our conscious awareness. This means the subconscious portion of the brain is always on and always filtering through the information and making judgment calls on what needs our immediate attention. Sometimes, that warning is nothing more than a vague "feeling" something's off. Always trust your gut and start asking questions.

In this gadget driven culture, people have forgotten to pay attention to body language gestures.

My experience is if a person doesn't "see" or "hear" anything "off", their "gut feeling" tends to be dismissed. For example, this is a "politically correct society" and if questioning the explanation or behavior would make the other person uncomfortable or look bad, the doubt often gets dropped. While a lot of people are no longer consciously noting body language cues, most people are reading body language gestures subconsciously and reacting to situations that appear "off." From a percentage standpoint, between the voice and "everything else" you're reacting to over 90% of the conversation which are non-verbals. Learn to trust yourself when you see and/or hear a body language cues that make you uncomfortable. More than likely, you are responding to a brief flash of emotion on the face, a sudden gesture, or your subconscious has already picked up on an inconsistency in the other person's story. When uncomfortable with a story, ask questions. There's nothing worse than thinking the story was "off" and you did nothing about it, only to find out later you were right.

Hear exactly what is being said

This is a simple but brilliant interviewing technique developed by Mark McClish, ex-law enforcement. He coined the technique "Statement Analysis." The approach calls for the interviewer to hear *exactly* what was said and question statements that don't sound right. The interviewer is never "to assume" anything, including the belief that the other party meant to say something else. Let me demonstrate:

> The interviewer is never "to assume" anything, including the belief that the other party meant to say something else.

- Human Resources, "You stated you were let go because the company thought you took the laptop. Did you take the laptop?"

- Candidate, "I took the laptop. I mean, I didn't take the laptop."

As the interviewer, it's your responsibility to recognize inconsistencies in the response and the fact that the candidate first admitted she took the laptop then changed her story. Don't forget to watch for changes to their baseline. Remember, lying causes stress on the body. Follow up in a neutral tone with a question such as:

- Human Resources: "You gave me a conflicting response to my question. Did you take the laptop?" or "It might be me... but I'm confused by your response, what happened to the laptop?"

By phrasing follow up questions in this manner, you remain neutral, you are not jumping to a conclusion and you're not accusing her of anything. Instead, you're letting the other party know you caught the inconsistency in her story and you are questioning the explanation. This also gives you more time to look and listen for additional body language gestures to support a conclusion.

Innocent people tell you they are innocent

Here's another tip I learned from law enforcement. When honest people are asked a question regarding to their innocence, and they're innocent, they immediately deny their involvement. On the other hand, dishonest people will attempt to "convince" you they're innocent by listing all the reasons why you shouldn't think they had anything to do with whatever you're looking into. For example, if an innocent person is asked, "Did you take the laptop?" Their response would be something along the lines of, "No I did not take the laptop." Or, "I didn't take the laptop." Notice, they deny any involvement immediately.

A dishonest person will feel the need to build a story around the question and they may or may not actually answer the question.

A dishonest person will feel the need to build a story around the question and they may or may not actually answer the question.

Here's a response I once received when I asked a female

employee about a missing laptop, "Which laptop? I've been having problems with my computer and the Help Desk hasn't been much help. Have you been having problems with the Internet? I'm not a computer person and I stay away from them. I don't fool with them." First of all, why does it matter which laptop is missing? A lap top is missing and I needed her to answer the question. Next she supplied me with a lot of irrelevant information. Lastly, she didn't answer the question, instead she talked around it.

Another approach dishonest people will take is to answer with a long winded response with a denial, but it's buried deep in the reply. Here's the same example using this technique: "Which laptop? I've been having problems with my computer and the Help Desk hasn't been much help. Have you been having problems with the Internet? I'm not a computer person and I stay away from them. I don't fool with them. Didn't take the laptop." The interviewee didn't deny involvement with the missing laptop until the very end of her statement. If there was no involvement, why did she wait so long to say she didn't take the laptop? Furthermore, why not admit your innocence up front? Don't let this technique throw you. Continue to ask additional questions until you believe you have enough information to make a determination on what happened to the lap top.

Auditory signs of stress

Auditory signs of stress deal with the voice. Once you get used to listening to the voice and hearing exactly what is said you will be able to hear

> Once you get used to listening to the voice and hearing exactly what is said you will be able to hear signs of stress in the person without even looking at them and over the phone.

signs of stress in the person without even looking at them and over the phone. When I had a territory that covered several states, it wasn't feasible for the company to fly me to a location every time there was complaint. As a result of this I became very good at listening to the other person's voice and picking up on changes to their voice baseline. Some of the changes I listened for are:

- Changes in their tone

- Change in volume
- Appearance of filler words and/or pauses
- Rate of speech

For example if a party was telling me what had occurred in a normal tone then the tone changed when she mentioned a certain co-worker (maybe it became harsh or sarcastic), I knew that was a red flag and I needed to find out more about the dynamics with the co-workers. Or if the person has no problem articulating what they wanted to say, then started to use filler words such as "uh, errr, hmmm" and introduced pauses. Use of these words gives the other party time to think about their responses. Sometimes they legitimately needed time to reflect (such as a minute detail) and I took that into consideration. However, when those appeared for no reason, I made a note to ask more questions. Probably the easiest one to catch is a person's rate of speech. It's easy to pick up their change of pace from fast to slow; slow to fast or either rate become an average speed.

Visual signs of stress

Visual signs of stress come in a variety of forms and can often take the form of a "quirk". For my purpose I will focus on four: pacifying behaviors, appearing smaller, movement, and no movement/freeze response.

> Visual signs of stress come in a variety of forms and can often take the form of a "quirk".

- <u>Pacifying behaviors</u>

Pacifying behaviors involve touch and are those quirky little responses a person has when they are under stress. Some examples are: lip biting, picking nails, arms crossed, hands clasped and/or hands being rubbed up and down the pant leg. These quirks are a bodily requirement, they sooth the body and are normal behavior when a person is nervous or stressed from a situation. Given what my role in the organization was (Human Resources), I was not surprised to see one or two of them when I met with folks; in fact I expected to see a few. These behaviors do not necessarily signal a "hot spot" unless they become excessive and/or cause bodily harm. For example if a person starts to pick at their nails as soon as they sit down, I consider that normal. Should she continue to pick her nails until she bleeds that's not normal and it would raise a red flag around the subject we had been discussing. Additionally, if she suddenly starts picking her nails after we have been talking for a while, that's a change in her baseline and would be a hot spot. For gentlemen, if they are sitting calmly with their hands clasped (normal for the situation), then they start to rub their hands on their pants leg, that's a red flag because they changed their behavior.

- Appearing smaller

A second response to stress is attempting to appear smaller. People use this behavior in an attempt to become a "smaller" target and draw less attention to themselves. Think of it this way, have you ever seen a dog who's been scolded? What does he do? He immediately shrinks his size in an attempt to "vanish" or become less of a target, then quietly slinks away. However, if you he's getting positive attention, he puffs up and doesn't mind calling attention to himself. Now take a look at the picture below. Assume Picture A is her baseline. Note the changes in Picture B – what do you see?

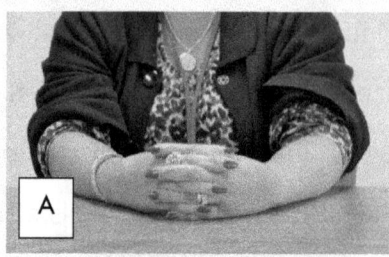

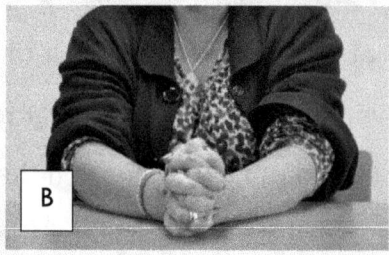

Notice the woman started out with a pacifying behavior (hands clasped). Once the stress began, not only is there tension in her now tightly clasped hands, but she also made hands and shoulders smaller.

- Movement

    Some body movement is natural and under stress, the body is looking for a way to decompress. One common release is "the jitters." Everyone has seen someone who can't seem to sit or stand still. This person is constantly in movement. It could be the person's natural state (i.e., baseline) or it could also be due to a medical condition. Always consider if there would be another reason for the behavior before concluding the person is nervous. Some of the more common movement gestures I tended to see are: bouncing legs, bouncing foot/feet, and/or playing with an object such as a pen. One of the most amusing interviews that involved "the jitters" concerned a woman with a click pen. She arrived with an outgoing personality, very well spoken, and a click pen for taking notes. She proceeded to click the pen throughout the interview. The clicking was very distracting and I almost asked her to give me the click pen, but my gut told me to "let it go." As I watched and listened to her I noticed after certain questions, the rate at which she clicked the pen would increase tenfold. That's when it struck me - that was her change in behavior! Once I recognized that, I knew exactly where to ask her more questions. By the end of the interview I was able to get her to tell me the real reason she left her last employer. She originally said it was a "mutual agreement" when in reality she had been asked to leave.   Professional pointer - when you need to get information from someone, give them a click pen, start asking questions, step back and see what happens!

- <u>Restricted/no movement and the freeze response</u>

Once you have determined what "jittery" behavior will be normal for the situation, it will be easier to notice sudden changes from movement to restricted movement, no-movement, or a freeze response. All of three are closely related and easy to spot. Remember some movement is normal and most people talk with their hands and arms. In most cases, restriction of movement is not normal. Here's an example, a candidate has been using her hands to describe and emphasize points in the story. All of a sudden you notice she is now sitting on her hands or one hand is being restrained from movement by the other. Here's the thing, when the body senses a threat, it will automatically start to pull in blood from areas that will not need energy and redirect it to areas that will need energy to "flee." In scientific terms, this is the body's freeze/fight/flight response that everyone has when dealing with danger. Restriction/no movement is an example of the body conserving energy so it can bolt from the room if the need arises.

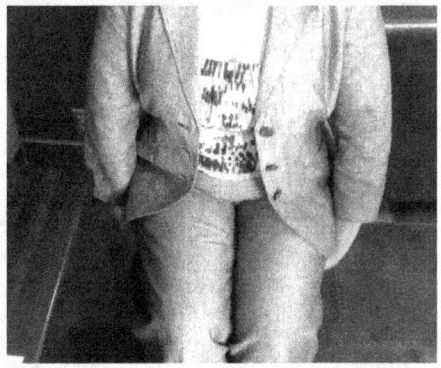

The freeze response (i.e. the deer in headlights look) is a sudden stop in movement. It occurs when the person is caught off guard and trying to figure out how to respond. Freeze responses can occur anywhere in the body and I think they are some of the easiest gestures to spot because they happen so quickly and are quite obvious. Some examples are: holding your breath, a look of surprise on the face, or hands/legs/feet are moving then suddenly stop. Below are two examples of the freeze response. In the face example, note the mouth hanging open and eyes are wide. The foot was kicking and now it's "frozen" and pointing straight up:

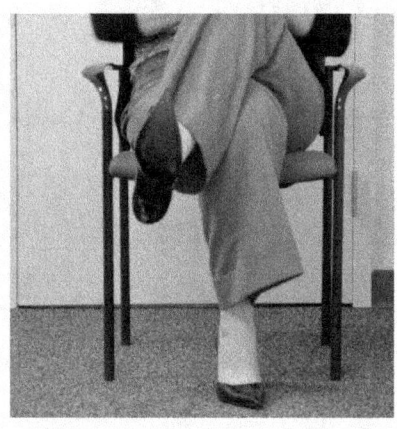

Bonus Section

Once again an effort not to confuse the reader, I am including a few extra tips that have helped me in the past.

Bonus Tip # 1: The person wants to exit the conversation

When we are completely engrossed in a conversation, our entire body faces the other party. However, when someone is uncomfortable with a conversation or ready to leave a conversation, their torso and/or foot will turn towards the nearest exit. For example, you stop your boss as she is walking down the hall and ask several questions. She stops and faces you as she answers the first couple of questions. As you continue to ask her questions, she starts to turn away. Make a note of her body language and let her out of the conversation. Tell her you will schedule a time to meet with her later or send her an email with your questions.

She will appreciate you letting her out of the conversation.

When this occurs in an interview, the party is usually sitting. It's easier to note the change in their torso instead of their feet. Below is a demonstration:

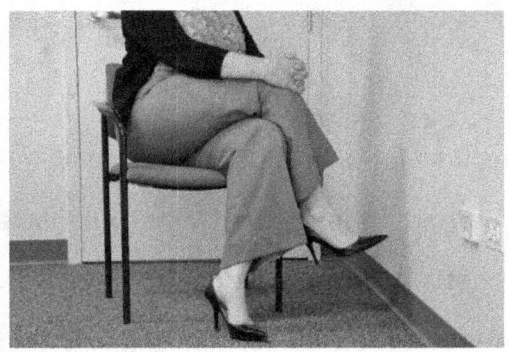

Blocking

Blocking behavior occurs when one party feels threatened or deeply impacted by a situation (i.e. a person covers their heart after witnessing something touching or tragic). There are two forms of blocking.

> Blocking behavior occurs when one party feels threatened or deeply impacted by a situation

The first form of blocking occurs when an object or a body part (think arms crossed) is placed between two parties. A second type of blocking involves the eyes and is seen as eye closure, blinking, or covering the eyes. By closing or covering the eyes, the person has a moment to block the offending object from sight for a second or two.

It was normal for me to witness both types of blocking whenever I had to address a serious matter. However, rather than wait for the behavior to occur I decided to develop my own case studies. Whenever I met with individuals, I would give them a bottle of water. I had two reasons for doing this, first if they were nervous and would drink the water, it would calm them down. Second, I want to see where they placed the water bottle. Here's how this works. Whenever you have lunch with someone and there are condiments or flowers in the middle of the table, what do you tend to do? You move them to the side so you can clearly see the other party. My thought was if this is true in a restaurant, it should be true in my office. Meaning I should be able to determine if when the other party is stressed out or relaxed based on where they place the water bottle. Sure enough, my water bottle placement theory was correct. If it was placed to the side that was a good sign - the other person didn't feel threatened by me. However, if the bottle was placed in between us I needed to work on getting the other party to relax. This was usually the case at the beginning of the interview. Lastly, if the water bottle mysteriously moves in between us as we talked, it was my red flag signal to evaluate the situation. Genius! It never failed.

Other object blocking behaviors I witnessed involved candidates picking up paperwork and holding it up vertically between the two of us. Both men and women would pick up personal objects (purse, briefcase, etc.) and placing them in their lap. From a body blocking perspective (i.e. using the body to block me) I used to witness arms becoming crossed, hands on the mouth, hands used as a stop sign. Last but not least were the eyes. I witnessed a lot of eye closure, blinking and covering of the eyes. Below is one example of a body block:

Top 5 Body Language Myths Revisited

Let's see how I did?

- I'm a mind reader;

- Body language isn't real;

- Body language is only gestures;

- One gesture tells the entire story;

- I can teach you to be a human lie detector;

Appendix A:
Tips for projecting a neutral and trustworthy personality

In order for people to open up and talk to you, they need to trust you. How you come across will influence how the other person responds to you. Always be aware of your baseline. To help you identify your baseline, I've included a checklist at the back of the book. You will need to work with a partner for approximately 5-days. For the first few days, you will be very aware that your partner is watching you and it will affect your normal baseline. After that you'll forget about them and revert back to your natural baseline. Depending on the situation, your baseline may need to change. For example, in an interview, you need to come across as open and neutral. However, if you're dealing with the outcome of a very serious matter, such as missing electronics or the dent in your car door, you may need to assume a more authoritative stance. You be the judge. Here are my tips for projecting a neutral and trustworthy person:

Body part	Behavior/Gesture
Head	Neutral with occasionally nodding up and down. A baseball should be able to fit between your chin and throat.
Facial Expression	Happy or neutral. Smile when appropriate throughout the conversation. If discussing a serious matter, smiling is not appropriate.
Eye Contact	40-60% of the time; use inverted triangle gaze area. The base of the triangle is the area between the outer edges of the eyes. At the edge of the eye draw a diagonal to the tip of the nose on both sides to create the triangle. Gaze should last no longer than 2-3 seconds; it can be held longer if you know the other party.
Voice	Neutral.
Rate of speaking	Match the other party's rate of speaking.

Handshake	Firm. Make eye contact and SMILE. Hands are palm to palm; three to four pumps.
Shoulders	Back but not rigid and facing the other party.
Arms	Arms by your side or bent at the waist.
Hands	Open, slightly curled, and in full view.
Torso	Facing the other party.
Feet	Both flat on the floor facing the other party. If standing, legs and feet flat with a comfortable stance between them.
Stance	Minimum of 6 inches apart.

Make sure your entire body is open to the other person. Any time the body is blocked by an arm, hands, paperwork, etc. it gives the impression the person is closed off.

Appendix B
What's my body language norm?

Body Part	When relaxed	Under pressure	What should I change it to?
How is the head held?			
When interacting with another, the head is?			
Does the head nod when interacting with another? If so,			

Body Part	When relaxed	Under pressure	What should I change it to?
how often?			
How is the forehead/brow positioned when interacting with another?			
How much eye contact is given?			

Body Part	When relaxed	Under pressure	What should I change it to?
Lips are what shape?			
Rate of speech when speaking?			
Tone of voice when speaking?			
Volume of voice			

Body Part	When relaxed	Under pressure	What should I change it to?
when speaking?			
Verbiage used when speaking?			
Neck position when interacting with another?			
Shoulders face which direction			

Body Part	When relaxed	Under pressure	What should I change it to?
when interacting with another?			
Posture when sitting?			
Posture when standing?			

How are the arms positioned when interaction with another?			
How are the hands positioned?			
Which way does the torso face when interacting with another?			
Which way do the legs face when			

interacting with another?			
Feet: 1. When sitting (flat, crossed, or one points towards the other) 2. When interacting to an employee?			
Does he/she touch blouse, shirt, tie, etc. when talking to another?			

When interacting with another, is there any facial touching?			
When walking what do both arms and hands do?			
Is the body constantly in motion?			

You Be the Expert — What Changed?

Before:

After:

_____

_____

Before:

After:

Answers to What Changed:

Before   After

Let's see who well you did:

Starting position	Change in position
Facing forward and leaning back.	Leaning slightly forward.

Head straight.	Head tilted to the left.
Wide hand gesture.	Wider hand gesture.
Hands/arms close to his head.	Hand/arms lower and closer to his chest.

Before   After

Let's see who well you did:

Starting position	Change in position
Head forward.	Head tilted.

No eye contact.	Eye contact.
No neck exposure.	Head tilted with neck exposed.
Lips straight/firm.	Pursed lips.
Arms/hands crossed.	Hands/arms uncrossed resting on the table.

Looking for a Speaker?

If you enjoyed Body Language for Success,

 Alicia Cuello is The Ideal Professional Speaker for Your Next Event!

Alicia Cuello will leave your audiences never looking at the world the same way. Alicia's high energy presentations engage and entertain the audience AND deliver a message that's dynamic and needed.

If you would like to learn more about booking Alicia for a keynote, breakout or workshop, please contact our office by calling 720.263.6101. You may also email your questions to Alicia@underlyingcommunications. Com.

Share this BOOK!

Quantity discounts are available. Call us for more information and a quote.

www.ingramcontent.com/pod-product-compliance
Lightning Source LLC
Chambersburg PA
CBHW071821200526
45169CB00018B/510